Title Deeds for Family Historians

Tim Wormleighton

THE FAMILY HISTORY PARTNERSHIP

Published by
The Family History Partnership
47 Bury New Road, Ramsbottom
Bury, Lancashire BL0 0BZ

First published 2012

© Tim Wormleighton

ISBN: 978 1 906280 35 2

Printed and bound by
Berforts Information Press
Southfield Road, Eynsham
Oxford OX29 4JB

CONTENTS

Introduction	5
What are Title Deeds?	6
Medieval Deeds	9
Post-Medieval Deeds	14
How to Recognise the Key Sections	26
Conclusion	30
Further Reading	32
Useful Websites	32
Addresses of Archive Repositories	32

Deeds safely stored in a deed box, the value to a family historian cannot be over estimated.

INTRODUCTION

At school I was always taught that it was one of the most cardinal of literary sins to begin any piece of writing on a particular subject with the words: *'there are many different kinds of ...'*. Yet, when discussing the fascinating but convoluted development of title deeds in England and Wales, there is little doubt that a more appropriate opening phrase would be difficult to find! The subject matter and context of title deeds are as varied as the human affairs they document, and this huge range of content and style may be one of the reasons why many people researching local or family history are reticent about using such records. Another must surely be the long-winded verbosity of their contents, which are clearly the products of the finest legal minds accustomed to using a dozen or more words where one would have been perfectly adequate! Nevertheless, title deeds can be readily understood with a little knowledge of their background and history and it is the aim of this booklet to provide the reader with the skills necessary to unlock their hidden secrets.

Title deeds represent the most widespread and numerous class of historical documents preserved in hundreds of archive repositories up and down the land. A brief foray into the *Access to Archives* website at **www.nationalarchives.gov.uk/a2a** will give a vivid picture of the sheer number and geographical spread of surviving records, as well as providing an idea of the bewildering range of agreements and contracts they document. Not surprisingly, then, there is plenty of scope for such records to provide invaluable information to supplement, or even fill gaps in, family trees. Where, for instance, a series of deeds exists for a particular property, a detailed picture of the changes in ownership or descent of that property through the generations can be assembled, often including dates of death of family members, details of the provisions of their wills and information on their children if, say, the estate was to be divided between them. A number of supplementary documents used to prove title are often found in bundles of deeds, including wills, certificates, examinations and, if one is fortunate, even detailed family pedigrees. Remember that a property did not necessarily have to be bought and sold to generate a series of title documents; items such as marriage settlements and family trust deeds can contain a wealth of information on family structure and relationships.

Many people tackling title deeds for the first time make a crucial, but quite understandable, mistake: they attempt to read the documents as they would a book or a letter, starting at the beginning and attempting to make it through to the end, and this is guaranteed to result in nothing more than confusion and frustration, for a large percentage of the text is, frankly, nothing more than legal verbiage. The key to the successful use of this source is to know exactly what to look for and where you are most likely to find it, for the basic format of the documents remains fairly standard over time, and once the key passages that actually contain the useful data can be identified, the salient information they hold may be extracted in a very short time. As with most archival sources, there is no substitute for actual 'hands on' experience of looking at as many different examples of deeds as possible, and the complexities of their contents should certainly not deter any family historian from including them on their 'to do' list.

WHAT ARE TITLE DEEDS?

Title deeds are written documents that record the fact that two or more people have reached an agreement concerning rights or property, usually a sale or transfer, that is to be legally binding. From the earliest times, a distinction was made between the way in which rights (called *incorporeal hereditaments*) and real estate (called *corporeal hereditaments*) were to be transferred. A simple **Deed of Grant** was used to convey incorporeal hereditaments, but the conveyance of real estate was a much more complicated business. Such estate could involve **freehold**, **leasehold** or **copyhold** tenure, and there could be more than one estate in a single property at the same time. For example, the owner of a freehold house could let his property to a tenant for a fixed period of time, and that tenant could, in turn, sub-let the property for a shorter period, resulting in three separate estates co-existing in the same property. Once created, such estates could only be terminated by proper legal process. Needless to say, the contents of deeds dealing with multiple estates in a single property can become very convoluted indeed!

The physical appearance of deeds and leases is distinctive. Nearly all were written on *parchment*, that is, treated animal skin, usually from sheep, which provides a remarkably robust and durable writing material. Even after the introduction of paper around 1500, parchment continued to be the material of choice for deeds through to the twentieth century. There is a marked difference in the size of medieval as opposed to post-medieval deeds, the former generally being much smaller and comprising a single sheet of parchment, whereas the latter often consist of several large sheets of parchment stitched together. The medieval deed would have been written out in duplicate, head to head, on a single sheet of parchment roughly A4 size. A lengthy word (often *'chirographum'*, the Latin for 'deed') or the letters of the alphabet were then written in the space between the two groups of text. The sheet of parchment was then cut in a wavy line through this middle section to produce two copies of the deed so that both parties to the agreement had their own copy. If there was any subsequent dispute as to the authenticity of the document the two halves could be reunited to form a perfect match and restore the cut-through word or letters written along the top edge of each (see Figure 1). The characteristic indented top edge of the medieval deed gave rise to the generic use of the word *'indenture'* to describe such documents, and later deeds retained this name, together with the indented edge, even though it no longer had the authenticating function of its medieval equivalent and was decorative only.

Many deeds did not have the indented top edge but rather a straight (or *'polled'*) top. This usually indicates that the document records some sort of unilateral declaration by an individual or group, rather than an agreement between parties. A familiar modern usage of this type of deed occurs when someone changes their name by 'deed poll'.

Space was left at the lower edge of the deed to allow for it to be folded upwards, forming a substantial base strip to take the signatures and/or seals of the parties involved. The seals, made from a mixture of beeswax and coloured resin, were impressed with the chosen signs of the parties, often from a signet ring. They could be either stuck direct to the folded base of the deed (*applied seal*) or hung by a thin strip of parchment

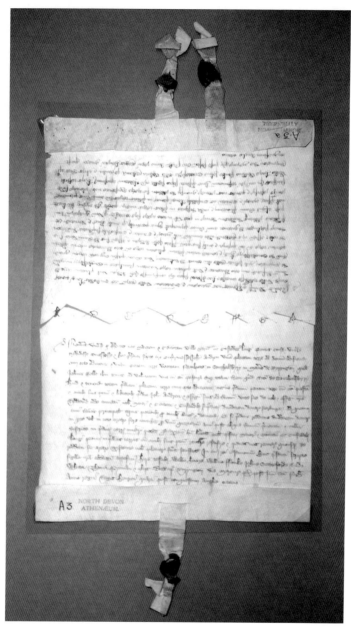

Figure 1. Indented deed with counterpart, 1407. Matching up the two parts of a medieval indenture recreates the hidden word or, as in this instance, the letters of the alphabet.

threaded through slits in the base (*appended seal*). Many medieval deeds have the seals of the parties only, as few people were literate enough to be able to sign their name.

MEDIEVAL DEEDS

There were two kinds of **freehold** estate (that is, property held indefinitely) in the medieval period: *fee simple* and *fee simple conditional*. The fee simple was an outright freehold estate with no strings attached; the property was conveyed to the buyer and '*his heirs and assigns for ever*' and passed to those heirs in accordance with recognised rules on the death of the owner, who was entitled to dispose of his property without any restriction. Fee simple conditional, on the other hand, restricted the descent of property to a specified class of heirs, for example male children only. Such property could originally be sold with limited freedom, but the statute clause *De Donis Conditionalibus* (literally, 'concerning conditional gifts') of 1285 made the sale of any such *'entailed'* property illegal. The idea behind this was to ensure that estates remained in the hands of the same family. However, as we shall see, some ingenious ways of facilitating the sale of entailed property were devised at a later date by exploiting loopholes in the legal system.

The most common way of transferring freehold property in the medieval period was by a process called *livery of seisin* (literally, 'delivery of possession'). This was a symbolic act of public transfer of a representative piece of the property being conveyed, usually a turf or a stick from the premises, presented to the buyer by the seller (or their representatives) in the presence of a number of witnesses. This process did not, in fact, require the creation of any written documentation to make it legally binding. The central point about livery of seisin was that it was a very public ceremony; the whole community witnessed the transaction and, in an age of small, insular communities, communal memory represented much better security than written documents few people would have been able to read.

The earliest deeds, termed **Feoffments** or **Deeds of Gift** (although this does not imply that no money changed hands), were merely created as a reminder that the livery of seisin ceremony had taken place, providing an additional element of security for the transaction. Consequently, these documents (in Latin) are always written in the past tense (look out for the phrase *'dedi, concessi et confirmavi'*, that is, 'have given, granted and confirmed'). They started to be widely used from the end of the twelfth century and were eventually abolished by the *Law of Property Act* of 1925, although, as we shall see, they had been largely superseded by other forms of deed long before that date (see Figure 2).

Another commonly encountered type of medieval deed is the **Quitclaim**, which was created to reinforce the security of a buyer's title to his new property. It typically records a disclaimer from an individual or a group of people (and their heirs) whom the buyer considered might file some sort of claim or interest in his property at some time in the future. This type of deed is readily identifiable by the inclusion of the phrase *'remisisse, relaxasse et quietclamasse'*, that is, 'have remised, released and quitclaimed', and the fact that the top edge of the document is usually straight, not indented (see Figure 3).

A further type of medieval deed is the **Fine** or **Final Concord**, which was the document produced at the conclusion of a pre-arranged court case brought by the buyer against the seller which was settled out of court in favour of the former. The resulting agreement, or *concord*, was written out in triplicate on a single, large sheet of parchment in the arrangement shown in Figure 4. The three copies were then cut out with a wavy line and the top two copies (called the left and right hand indentures) given to the respective parties to the sale. The remaining copy, the **foot**, was retained as unassailable evidence of title by the court. The most popular court for hearing such proceedings was the Court of Common Pleas at Westminster. The National Archives houses the series of **Feet of Fines** from this court (TNA CP 25) dating from 1182, and many counties have published transcripts of the documents relating to their area.

Medieval deeds are almost always written in Latin, usually heavily abbreviated. They rarely include any dating clause before the late thirteenth century, although it is often possible to deduce an approximate date by the style of the handwriting and the names of the witnesses listed at the end of the document. When the inclusion of dating becomes customary, it is usually done by reference to saints' days or

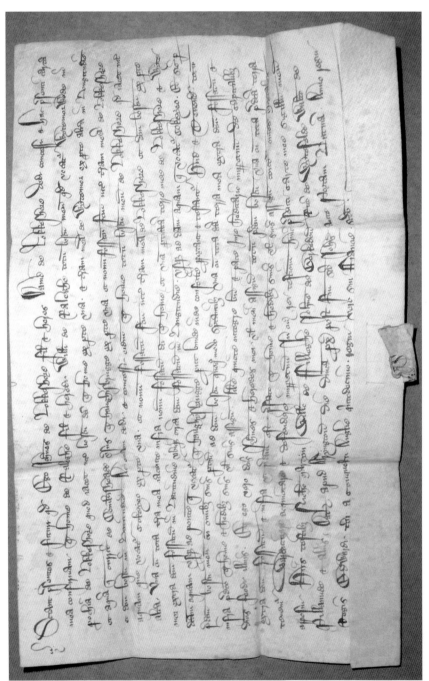

Figure 2. Feoffment, 1341. This type of deed was created to record the fact that the livery of seisin ceremony to transfer property had taken place, and was therefore written in the past tense.

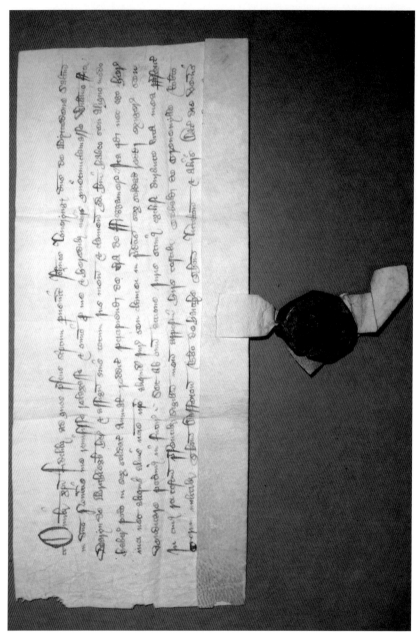

Figure 3. Quitclaim, 1371. A common form of medieval deed recording a disclaimer of interest in a right or property by one or more persons, often the seller(s).

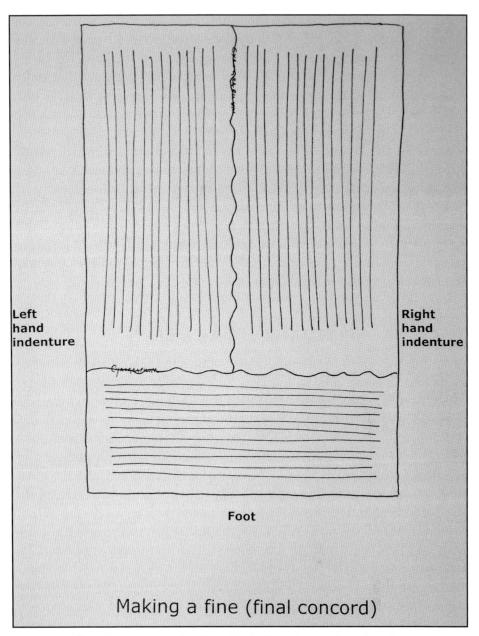

Figure 4. The three parts of a fine, the left and right hand indentures and the foot below these, were cut from a single piece of parchment. As with the indenture, the respective parts could be fitted together to authenticate the documents.

festivals, for example 'the Monday after the Feast of the Nativity of St John the Baptist', and the year is usually recorded as a regnal year, for example 'the twelfth year of the reign of Edward II'. The difficulties associated with *palaeography,* the deciphering of old writing, can usually only be resolved through a combination of practice and experience, but, fortunately for those of us who struggle with reading and translating medieval Latin, the text of such documents is short compared with later deeds, and the layout of the contents is fairly standard. Most record offices holding collections of medieval deeds have produced calendars or catalogues describing the individual documents in some detail, and many of these are now available on the *Access to Archives* website at **www.nationalarchives.gov.uk/a2a.** Help and advice on reading Latin documents is readily available both in print (see Further Reading section) and online. For example, **www.nationalarchives.gov.uk/records/reading-old-documents.htm.**

POST-MEDIEVAL DEEDS

Although there were undoubted advantages in making the transfer of freehold property public knowledge, the downside was that one's feudal superiors were fully aware of all such transactions, and were thus able to exact the maximum amount of financial benefit ensuing, mainly *relief,* which was a payment owed to the lord of the manor by anyone inheriting property within his domain. It was therefore only natural that people would try to find ways of evading such payments, and the most successful ploy was for the seller to make livery of seisin to a large group of people who agreed to hold the property *'for the use of'* the actual owner. As there was no likelihood of this entire group dying at the same time, no relief could actually be claimed. The resulting loss of earnings was considerable, and it was especially bad for the Crown, which held the largest number of manors. As a result, legislation called the *Statute of Uses* was introduced in 1535 declaring that the person for whom a use was raised was henceforth to be considered the proper legal owner of the property and, as such, wholly responsible for any feudal dues that may be owing.

The effect of this legislation was far reaching: it broke the long-established association between the livery of seisin ceremony and the transfer of property ownership. For if seisin could now be granted to a person or group of people who were no longer considered in law to be the owner or owners of the property concerned, the livery of seisin ceremony was, in effect, relegated to the role of an antiquated sideshow; what mattered now was the actual exchange of money from buyer to seller. Of course, this meant that a public display of transfer no longer had any real legal significance and increased the need for the creation of proper title deeds to record sales. In order to maintain public knowledge of property transfers and to prevent secret conveyancing, the *Statute of Enrolments* was passed in the same year, requiring all such transfers of freehold property to be by legally constructed deed enrolled in the Royal Courts (recorded on the Close Rolls, TNA C 54) or with the local Quarter Sessions courts (records of which are in county record offices). Out went the feoffment deed and the livery of seisin ceremony and in came a new type of deed, called the **Bargain and Sale,** to reflect this change in conveyancing practice (see Figure 5). The characteristic phrase in these documents, which are generally written in English, is 'grant, bargain and sell'. Many people continued to employ livery of seisin as an alternative public statement of sale, however, and recorded the fact on the back, or *dorse*, of the deed. Such a document is referred to as a **Bargain and Sale with Feoffment** but, unlike the medieval feoffment, this type of deed was written and signed in advance of the ceremony. Such deeds were not normally enrolled. Occasionally, deeds of bargain and sale are encountered without any endorsement of enrolment or livery of seisin; rather than implying that neither event took place, these items are normally counterpart duplicates on which it was not considered necessary to record such details.

With the profound social changes brought about by the decline of the feudal system and the growth of private land ownership in the Tudor period, property owners were no longer content to have their transactions held up to public scrutiny as they had been in the past. As a consequence, their lawyers were encouraged to devise a new method of conveying property that would allow them to do so privately yet remain within the letter of the law. The resulting procedure, introduced around 1610, was so ingenious and so successful that it became the

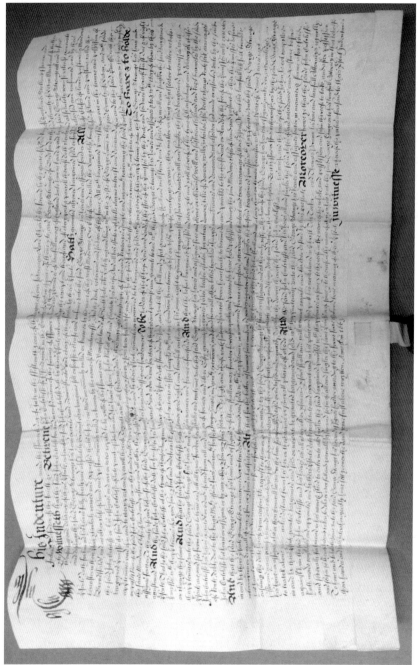

Figure 5. Bargain and sale, 1663. This type of deed replaced the medieval feoffment as the livery of seisin ceremony fell out of use.

method of choice for most property transfers right up to the middle of the nineteenth century, when the *Statute of Uses* was repealed and private conveyancing was officially accepted through the introduction of the modern **Conveyance**. A seller of property would lease it to the prospective buyer for the period of one year which, under the terms of the *Statute of Uses*, raised a use in favour of the buyer who was therefore deemed to be in actual possession of the property. Under Common Law, the seller could then relinquish his future (or *reversionary*) interest in the property to the buyer, who thus became its outright owner. As neither part of this transaction technically represented a freehold interest, the legal requirement to publicly declare the sale by enrolment or any other means was cleverly evaded. This arrangement, known as the **Lease and Release**, involved the drawing up of two separate documents, the **Lease for a year** and a larger and more detailed **Release** dated the following day. Often, the smaller lease will be found tucked inside its larger companion (see Figure 6), but frequently the two will have parted company over the years and only one part survives. A stray lease of this type can, however, be easily distinguished from a genuine lease for a year by the inclusion of the phrase 'bargain and sale', the nominal consideration (usually five shillings), a peppercorn rent and a phrase towards the end stating that the 'intent and purpose' of the lease is that the buyer 'may be in actual possession'.

The post-medieval lawyers also developed equally ingenious methods of enabling owners to sell *entailed* property tied up in family trusts, something that had been illegal since the thirteenth century. Family settlements or trusts were increasingly common from the seventeenth century on, to ensure that estates remained within the family by making it impossible for one individual member to sell them off. Although this resulted in security, it also meant that no part of an estate could be legally sold to raise capital for improvements. In order to get round this, lawyers developed two popular methods of conveying entailed land, both of which involved pre-arranged, collusive court cases.

The first was the **Fine** or **Final Concord**, which, as we have seen, had been used as a straightforward way of transferring property throughout the medieval period. By this method, the buyer of a property (called the

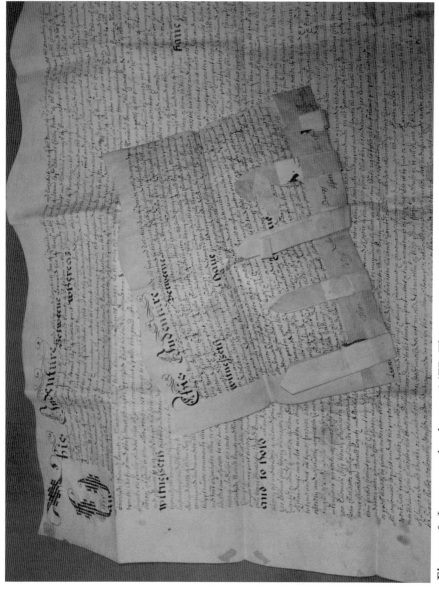

Figure 6. Lease and release, 1675. This two part deed became the preferred method of transferring property as it avoided the requirement for public registration.

plaintiff or *querent*) brought a court case against the seller (called the *deforciant*), with his agreement, alleging that he had agreed to sell him the property in question but had failed to do so. Before the court could reach its judgement, the two came to an out of court settlement whereby the seller acknowledged that the property should rightfully belong to the buyer. The reason this charade was followed is that by taking out such a case in the courts, the buyer was awarded the property in fee simple, even if the land was previously subject to an entail. Three copies of the resulting document were made, just as in the medieval period, and the foot retained by the court as evidence of title. Unfortunately, fines themselves (see Figure 7) do not provide much detailed information on the property being sold; usually, the description is limited to nothing more informative than a house and so many acres of land in a particular parish. Even the amount of money paid for the property is usually recorded as a standard figure that bears little resemblance to the amount that actually changed hands. However, they were often accompanied by a companion **Deed to Lead to (or Explain) the Uses of a Fine**, which does often provide more specific details of the transaction.

Whereas the fine was said to be 'levied', the other popular method of conveying entailed land, the **Common Recovery**, was said to be 'suffered'. This also involved a fabricated lawsuit in the courts, in which the buyer (called the *demandant*) brought an arranged case against the seller (called the *tenant-in-tail*) to 'recover' the property being sold, claiming that it was rightfully his and that he had been wrongly ejected from it by a third party (a wholly fictitious individual normally given a stock name such as Hugh Hunt or Richard Rowe). The seller, instead of 'defending' the case in person, called upon another (called the *vouchee*) to stand up for him. Following the pantomime protocol of such cases, the buyer would then ask to consult (or *imparl*) with the vouchee out of court. Both then left the court for a brief period, but while the buyer returned the vouchee did not, and he was thus held to be in contempt of court. The seller's case therefore collapsed and the buyer was awarded the property in fee simple, even if it was previously entailed, just as with the fine. In its developed form, the recovery case was often brought against the seller's lawyer or agent, to whom the property had been previously assigned by a **Deed to Make a Tenant to the Precipe** (*'precipe'*

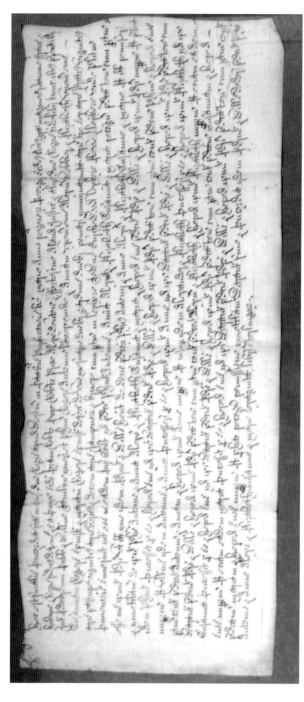

Figure 7. Left hand indenture of a fine, 1729. The collusive court action used in the medieval period was adopted at a later date to effect a method of transferring entailed property.

Figure 8. Exemplification of a common recovery, 1703. Like the fine, the common recovery was a collusive court procedure frequently used to transfer entailed property. The resulting document, the exemplification, is a rather grand looking deed sealed with a Great Seal.

being the first word of the relevant court action). The written record resulting from this legal fiction was an **Exemplification of a Common Recovery**, a rather grand looking document sealed with the court seal (see Figure 8). Most cases were heard by the Royal Court of Common Pleas in Westminster, and its documents are sealed with the Great Seal of the reigning monarch (see Figure 9). Like the fine, the details provided by such deeds are sketchy. Furthermore, court documents were written in Latin up to 1733 and in a peculiar handwriting style called 'common-law hand' that appears at first sight virtually impossible to decipher. Fortunately, most record offices have extracted the useful information from such items in their catalogue systems. Details of recoveries were recorded on the **Plea Rolls** (TNA CP 40) and, later, **Recovery Rolls** (TNA CP 43) held by The National Archives. This convoluted method of conveying entailed property was in general use from the late fifteenth century through to 1833, when, together with the fine, it was rendered obsolete by an Act that, mercifully for both buyers and sellers alike, permitted such property to be sold by a simple disentailing deed.

Family trusts were, nevertheless, a commonly used way of ensuring that property remained in the same family down the generations, and the documents associated with them, generally called **Settlements**, are therefore of prime importance for family historians. A property owner wishing to set up a family trust would arrange to convey his property to a body of trustees, normally his friends or relations, who agreed to hold it on his behalf during his lifetime, then in trust for specified heirs. Such settlements were often drawn up at the time of a marriage or when children reached the age of majority and a revised settlement may have been made for each generation. They can contain an enormous amount of detail of family relationships, ages, occupations, and so on, and may even include associated documentation such as wills or family trees. The reason they go into so much detail was the need to ensure that the property remained in the hands of a body of trustees rather than fall into the possession of any member of the family, who would then have been able to sell it off. A marriage settlement included an arrangement for the payment of an annual income, or *annuity*, for the owner's wife, with adequate provision for her should she outlive her husband, and details of portions to be allocated to any children of the marriage. Most

Figure 9. Great Seal from a common recovery. Typically, the Great Seal depicts the reigning monarch seated on the throne on one side and on horseback on the other.

documents go into great depth, providing solutions to cover every eventuality of life. In some settlement deeds, part of the estate was intentionally left out of the terms of the arrangement, affording the possibility of raising a mortgage on it or selling it to raise capital at some time in the future. The most popular way of effecting a family settlement was by the **Lease and Release** method described above.

The **Mortgage** was a popular method of raising capital in past centuries, and the ability to recognise its appearance in collections of title deeds, which may not always be immediately obvious, will ensure the avoidance of considerable confusion. Nowadays, we take out a mortgage with a bank or building society to secure a loan in order to buy a house. However, this is a fairly recent development. In past centuries, a mortgage was generally taken out on property that was already in the borrower's ownership as the security for a cash loan from another individual. The deed recording this arrangement looks, to all intents and purposes, like a regular **Bargain and Sale** or **Lease and Release** and appears to show the conveyance of the property concerned to the lender. However, the property is usually conveyed for a fixed term of years, sometimes as much as several thousand years, rather than indefinitely, and towards the end of the text there will be some reference to the ability of the borrower to redeem his property by the repayment of the loan and any interest accruing, usually including the telling phrase *'equity of redemption'*. The property did not, in actual fact, change hands at all and the borrower continued to enjoy full possession. It was transferred to the lender for an abstract term only, but the deed usually includes a clause giving the lender the right to enter into the property or put it up for sale should the borrower default on his repayments at any time. Often the mortgage includes a *defeasance* clause, which states that the terms of the deed will be considered null and void if the loan is repaid by an agreed date. Subsequent arrangements could be made by which the mortgage was transferred to a new lender if the original one needed to call in his debts. These would have been recorded in an **Assignment of Mortgage** deed. The lengthy terms of years involved in many mortgage arrangements were not necessarily extinguished by the repayment of the loan. Deeds are commonly found recording the assignment of a long term of years to an individual who was to hold the property *'in trust to* *attend the inheritance'* for a property owner who had paid off his debt; often the original mortgage is referred to and there is usually a nominal consideration of five shillings. Such an arrangement may form part of a larger deed if the property is being sold at the same time. Sometimes, a separate **Bond**, or promise, to repay the loan by a certain date may be found with the mortgage deed. Additional funds could be borrowed on the security of the property, either by **Further Charge** from the existing lender or with separate mortgages from new lenders, provided that the total amount borrowed did not exceed the estimated value of the property. A memorandum of **Reconveyance**, recording the repayment in full, may be written on the back of a cancelled mortgage deed.

In contrast to the freehold, which was held forever or indefinitely, **leasehold** property was held for a fixed period of time in return for an initial consideration and an annual payment of rent to the owner of the property. The term was fixed either in years, the duration of the lives of named individuals, or a combination of the two. **Leases for years** set a definite limit on the length of the lease, for example ten years. Leases for very long periods, such as a thousand years, are sometimes encountered and in such cases the possibility that a mortgage is involved should be considered. **Leases for lives** of named individuals were, by their nature, of an uncertain duration, and were often thought of as virtual freeholds, as new lives could be substituted on the death of one of those named in the lease upon payment of a fee (usually called a *heriot* or *farlieu*). A common form of lease used in the south west of England combined a term of years, usually ninety nine, with three named lives, and there is evidence to suggest that this arrangement largely replaced the manorial *copyhold* system from the end of the medieval period. It provided advantages for both landlord and tenant: the landlord retained his freehold interest, while the tenant enjoyed greater security of tenure and the ability to sub-let the property. Most leases of this type were converted to simple ninety year leases by the *Law of Property Act* of 1925, but many had already been surrendered in the nineteenth century, when high initial payments meant that tenants had little money left to invest in the properties they occupied.

Copyhold was the ancient form of manorial tenure, whereby property was considered to be held either from a feudal lord directly or from one of his subordinates. Such property could be bought and sold, mortgaged or bequeathed just like a freehold estate, but any changes of occupation or ownership were administered through the manorial court and thus recorded on the **Court Roll**, a copy of the relevant entry being produced as the equivalent of a title deed, hence the term *'copyhold'* (see Figure 10). In order to transfer a manorial property, it would first have to be 'surrendered' to the lord of the manor, who then formally 'admitted' the new owner or tenant. When property descended down the generations of a single family, the importance of this type of record for the family historian is obvious, particularly as manorial court rolls represent one of the few locally held sources that pre-date parish registers. The downside is that medieval manorial records were written in heavily abbreviated Latin requiring considerable interpretation. Copyhold tenure was not formally abolished until 1922, when most surviving holdings were converted to freeholds. Owing to their importance as a unique record of land ownership, manorial records represent one of the few categories of historical records in England and Wales to enjoy some degree of statutory protection. The **Manorial Documents Register** was established in 1922 to record the extent and location of all such records, and is the essential finding aid for researchers. Many collections of manorial records will be found in the appropriate county record office, although others may have migrated, with their owners, to different parts of the country at some time in the past.

HOW TO RECOGNISE THE KEY SECTIONS

As stated at the outset, the secret to the successful use of title deeds lies in the ability to pick out the sections containing the important information from the general mass of strangely written words that stretch from one side of the parchment to the other in interminable, soporific lines that have very little punctuation to provide assistance. Once the contents can be decoded in this way, it is often possible to produce a comprehensive summary of the significant data in a relatively short time. If you know what to look for, and where it is likely to appear in the document, using these records becomes far more straightforward.

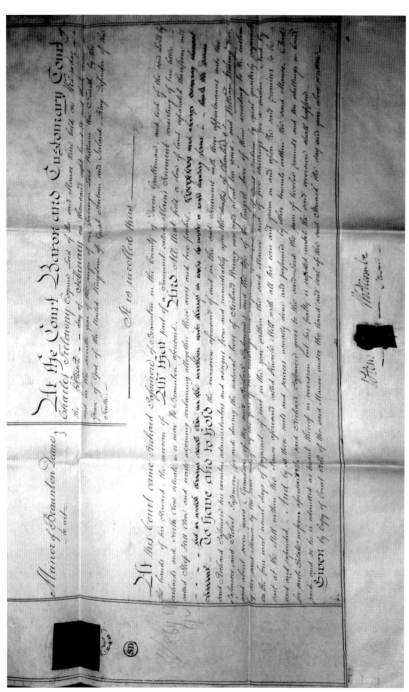

Figure 10. A late example of a copyhold deed, 1837. Copyhold was an ancient form of manorial tenure, so named because the title deed produced was literally a copy of the relevant entry from the court roll. It was abolished in 1922.

When considering post-medieval deeds, the identification of the key passages is usually made easier by the fact that they are introduced by large, bold lettering. Most can be divided into the following sections identified in that way:

Introduction, beginning 'THIS INDENTURE...' This section includes the dating clause. The initial letter of the deed is often decorated in some way.

Names of the parties, beginning 'BETWEEN...' This section gives the names, occupations and places of residence of those involved in the recorded agreement. There can be any number of parties to a deed, and a party can consist of several individuals. An individual can also belong to more than one party.

Recitals of previous transactions, beginning 'WHEREAS...' There may be several such sections. Do not be tempted to skip over them, as they often contain useful information from previous deeds to place the present agreement in context.

Terms of the present agreement, beginning 'NOW THIS INDENTURE WITNESSETH...' This section is the actual meat of the deed itself, describing the property being transferred and the amount of money changing hands. There may be more than one such section in a very complicated arrangement.

Duration of the agreement, beginning 'TO HAVE AND TO HOLD...' This will be forever for a freehold property, or a specified term for a lease or mortgage. It will also give details of any additional conditions or restrictions.

Witness clause, beginning 'IN WITNESS THEREOF...' The formal conclusion of the document that acknowledges its signing and sealing by the parties concerned.

Sometimes the deed will include **marginal additions**, such as plans (particularly of urban properties), schedules of previous deeds or lists of lands affected by the agreement.

Also take a look at things that have been written on the back of the deed. These are called **endorsements**, and include receipts of money and interest payments, memoranda of subsequent transactions and confirmation of enrolments. Often, once the deed had been folded up, a summary of its contents was written on the outside (see Figure 11). The

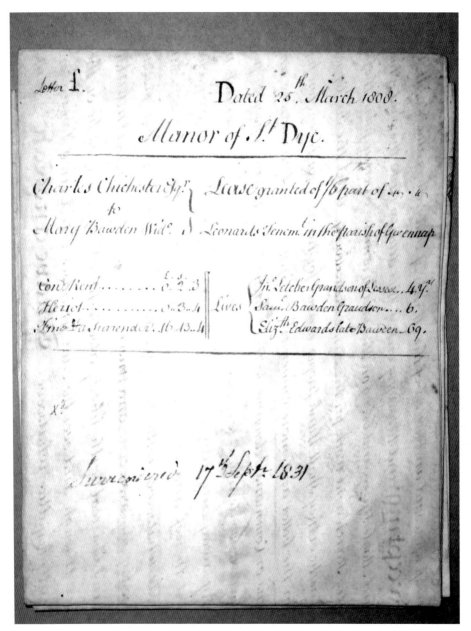

Figure 11. Endorsed description on lease, 1808. Endorsements frequently provide a useful summary of the contents of a deed or lease.

amount of detail given varies considerably but sometimes all the relevant data contained in a deed is recorded in this way.

When a property was put up for sale in the eighteenth or nineteenth century, the seller's solicitor would assemble all the previous deeds and related documents as evidence of the seller's title, forming a bundle of related deeds that would then pass to the new owner. As part of this process, an **Abstract of Title**, containing summaries of all the previous deeds, would be drawn up, and these often provide the best starting point for the researcher confronted with a large sequence of deeds for a property.

Remember that much of the hard graft of transcribing, translating and cataloguing the contents of title deeds has already been undertaken by the staff of most record offices and libraries. This is particularly true of medieval deeds, which are often described in great detail, saving hours of work needed to decipher the heavily abbreviated Latin originals. Often, the catalogues of collections of deeds may provide all the information required without having to resort to tackling the original documents at all. As mentioned above, a look at the *Access to Archives* website at **www.nationalarchives.gov.uk/a2a** will provide a good overview of the sort of catalogue information that is available.

CONCLUSION

The lack of any statutory protection for title deeds (although there are measures covering manorial documents) has meant that the family historian must be prepared to search far and wide for surviving material relating to his or her area of interest. Often, the local record office or library is only one link in a chain of repositories that stretches to the national institutions like the British Library or The National Archives in London, other record offices and libraries, museums, private custodians and even other countries. Attention should be drawn in this respect to the work of the **National Register of Archives (www.nationalarchives.gov.uk/nra)**, which maintains a database on the location of estate and family archives, and the **Manorial Documents Register (www.nationalarchives.gov.uk/mdr)** through which collections of manorial documents may be located. Both are based at The

National Archives at Kew. Local deed registries exist for many areas, including the Yorkshire ridings, Middlesex and Hampshire. In recent years, the growth of the Internet as a research tool has made the task of tracking down information on the survival and location of historical records much easier, and all major repositories now have comprehensive websites or online catalogues available to search in the comfort of your own home. It is also worth checking out academic websites, such as the University of Toronto's *Deeds Project* **(www.utoronto.ca/deeds)** or the University of Nottingham's *Deeds in Depth* **(www.nottingham.ac.uk/manuscriptsandspecialcollections/researchguidance/deedsindepth/introduction.aspx).**

Regrettably, a series of deeds charting the ownership history of a single property will often have been split, usually when a large estate has been sold off piecemeal or otherwise broken up in the past. In addition, the *Law of Property Act* of 1925 ended a buyer's right to all previous title deeds and this, coupled with the subsequent introduction of the land registration system that renders all such documents of no legal significance, has led to a considerable dispersal of records. The **British Records Association (www.britishrecordsassociation.org.uk)** has been extremely active in rescuing endangered collections of deeds and depositing them in appropriate repositories and has done much to raise awareness of their importance as a research resource among owners and solicitors, but there are still, unfortunately, occasions when unique and irreplaceable historical records are destroyed through ignorance or neglect. Nevertheless, with a little patience and more than a smattering of good fortune, the family historian has much to gain from investigating these sources, and the information they provide can often supplement or make good data gleaned from the more familiar genealogical records. As we have seen, there may be a greater degree of interpretation required in extracting that information, but the potential gems that the documents can reveal, combined with their vast numbers, ensure that title deeds and leases will always represent an important element in the wide range of original source material preserved for posterity and accessible in archive repositories across the land, and one that will repay handsomely the exploration of the intrepid family historian.

FURTHER READING

A. A. Dibben, *Title Deeds, 13th-19th Centuries* (The Historical Association,1971)

N. W. Alcock, *Old Title Deeds: a guide for local and family historians* (Phillimore, 1986)

J. Cornwall, *How To Read Old Title Deeds, 16th-19th Centuries* (University of Birmingham, 1964)

E. A. Gooder, *Latin for Local History* (Longmans, 1961)

D. Stuart, *Latin for Local and Family Historians* (Phillimore, 2006)

H. Marshall, *Palaeography for Family and Local Historians* (Phillimore, 1999)

C. T. Martin, *The Record Interpreter* (Phillimore, 1982)

C. R. Cheney, *Handbook of Dates for Students of English History* (Royal Historical Society, 1970)

USEFUL WEBSITES

The National Archives: **www.nationalarchives.gov.uk**
Access to Archives: **www.nationalarchives.gov.uk/a2a**
National Register of Archives: **www.nationalarchives.gov.uk/nra**
Manorial Documents Register: **www.nationalarchives.gov.uk/mdr**
British Records Association: **www.britishrecordsassociation.org.uk**
The British Library: **www.bl.uk**

ADDRESSES OF ARCHIVE REPOSITORIES

See the ARCHON directory at **www.nationalarchives.gov.uk/archon**